Previous Books by Jerry Schaefer

Guide to Swifter and Deeper Thoughts (1987, unavailable)

Women: Down through the Ages, How Lies Have Shaped Our Lives
(2007, reprinted 2022)

The Story of You (2019)

Cruising through the Teens, Easier Than It Seems (2021)

Isn't it Kind of Funny That… (2022)

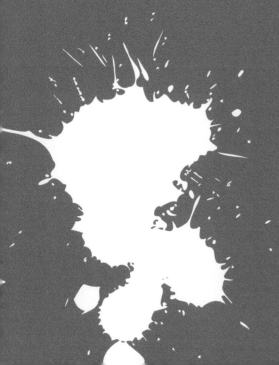

LOOK INSIDE
www.expandjoy.com

From Patriarchy to Paradise

(It's about time)

by **Jerry Schaefer**

Illustrated by **Gabriel Berrón**

Cut Bank
Penguin
Pubs

164 Argonne Avenue #1
Long Beach CA 90803

From Patriarchy to Paradise
(It's about time)

ISBN: 979-8-218-53895-8

Illustrated by Gabriel Berrón ~ www.imagencontacto.com

Layout/production by Anne Pace ~ pace@vermontel.net

Edited by Melinda Tourangeau ~ practicalconversations.org

First Edition

November 2024

To women–

For 8,000 years you've been
expecting, awaiting new life to
emerge from the ashes of patriarchy.
The time is up.
No need to wait.
Let's celebrate.

What does our story consist of?

One of the important pieces in anyone's story is sex, male or female. Whichever one you are at birth, patriarchy will be a major influence. Sex, with it's peculiar patriarchal stamp, weaves its way through our stories.

We have spent most of our time on earth as hunter-gatherers. Towards the end of that one-to-two-million-year period, we began to use words that evolved into sentences, and we had the first "pictures" (thoughts) in our heads. The Agricultural Revolution, 8 to 10,000 years ago, accelerated these developments. That's where patriarchy had its beginnings. Patriarchy accompanied civilization. Since the dawn of recorded history, we've lived under the aegis of patriarchy.

This book is about our story, how we have fared under patriarchy. It is still ongoing, in the works, we are far from finished. It can only get better (it might get a bit worse first). That's exciting.

~~~

Contents

PART ONE
Early History

THE CURIOUS STORY OF

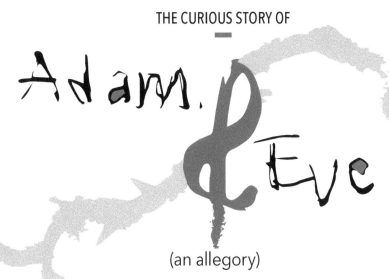

(an allegory)

Chapter 1

Adam and Eve had everything they could possibly want in the fabled garden of Eden. Except for one thing, the knowledge of good and evil. They could only obtain that by eating fruit from the forbidden tree.

Eve picked a forbidden apple, took a bite, then, with a twinkle in her eye (already the apple working its magic), she offered it to Adam. How could he resist?

Out they went! God clearly "lost it." He told them to leave and don't come back. Eve began feeling future womb pains, and Adam was wiping imagined sweat from his furrowed brow.

The garden was clearly a set-up. The forbidden tree dwarfed everything else in the garden. Neon lights blinked on every branch, each apple sparkled and sent out scented, enticing aromas. Yes, they could eat anything they wanted, but obviously the only really worthwhile edible in the garden was the one thing they couldn't have.

People have always blamed them for messing things up for us, their progeny. But who among us would not have done the same thing? We might've eaten two apples! To be twice as smart.

Naturally, we'd be curious. What is this "knowledge" thing? And "good and evil"?

Who wouldn't just have to know?!

When God came around for the daily inspection, he noticed right away that an apple was missing. He also noticed Adam and Eve were hiding because they were naked. Now they knew it! Because the apple gave them knowledge. And they were ashamed (at being naked, not for stealing the apple).

God questioned Adam about the purloined apple.
Adam blamed Eve for tempting him. Eve blamed the
snake for deceiving her. The snake slithered away
silently, destined to eat dirt all the days of his life.
And to be heeled by Eve.

God told Eve that she would henceforth be under
her husband's power, and he would have dominion
over her.

Hence was scripted the simple plot line for men
to be able to satisfy their natural lust. Guilt free.
No liability.

OUR EARLY STORY

gatherers

Chapter 2

For 90% of our human history, our way of life was that of hunter-gatherers. The hunter-gatherer is still part of us, in our blood. Incidentally, now we forage on the Internet...

That way of life was quite simple. We foraged for nuts, seeds, plants, and roots to eat. We lived in teepees and makeshift huts for a few days or weeks, until we needed to move on to a better "store." During that time, men hunted animals for meat and the women nursed the babies. Women also nursed the fire (because if the fire went out, there were no matches lying around), waiting till their men came back to the camp to cook the catch.

But in the early days, when we first came down out of the trees, it took us roughly 20,000 to 50,000 years to learn to walk upright. It took a little longer for women as they had the added weight of breasts and babies.

While still living in the trees (in the pre-hunter-gatherer period), we had a communication system similar to what chimpanzees and apes have today. They look at us today and probably wonder where we went wrong.

Our chirps and whistles and groans served to warn of danger and to signal when dinner would be served.

Keep in mind, we had two and a half million years to get from just-another-group-of-baboons-in- the-trees to becoming a distinct humanoid population. A long time, but well spent.

Let's spend a little time "there" since there's a part of us that's still there. Our bodies are probably fairly similar, we still have our reptilian brain if we need it, and we still have our "fight or flight" mechanisms intact.

We did not exactly hit the ground running. In fact, there were probably some groups/families that decided to ditch the ground life and take to the trees again. Or they never came down. These would have been the fish that stayed in the ocean instead of venturing onto dry land.

Keep in mind, at this point there is very little to distinguish us from other animals.

There were numerous humanoid-like creatures wandering around and it would be many years before a distinct type of humanoid (that would become us) began to become dominant.

During that time, if the chimpanzees or bonobos were having a party, we could have slipped in without having to show our ID.

At this time, we were just like animals. Some animals ate plants exclusively. Others ate mainly meat. We were an animal that ate both. Different animals excelled in different areas: speed, agility, strength. We were a work in progress.

We worshiped some plants because of their life-giving properties. We recognized the power of the sun to grow our plants and we subsequently revered it.

Looking about for a God to give thanks to, what better candidate then the sun!

STORY OF THE
—

Agricultural Revolution

Chapter 3

The Agricultural Revolution was a major turning point in human history. About 10,000 BCE, humans began to cultivate crops and domesticate goats. This was a big change from the system of hunter-gatherers that had prevailed for over a million years.

By 8500 BCE, the Middle East was home to many permanent villages, primarily farmers. The Agricultural Revolution enabled increasing food production. With this innovation, more human life could be sustained. This advent increased the population and turned the villages into cities—the rise of the Mesopotamian civilization.

Early centuries of man were taken up by conflict. Blame it on agriculture. Early peoples realized that by putting seeds into the ground, rather than relying on nature to let those seeds drop when dry, they got a lot more grain.

Civilization was about to begin. A way of life that made them quite *uncivil* towards each other.

Soon they were putting in more and more seeds into the ground, making more land available for planting, and harvesting more and more grain. More-More-More…so began the ruthless pursuit of More.

For the first time, they had more than they needed in a day. The first surplus. What to do with it? "We need a place to put it, we need to keep track of it, we need to protect it from other tribes, need to keep records, we need soldiers to protect it, we need an army, we need somebody to keep track of the army, we need somebody to oversee the army we need…" Here comes bureaucracy, accompanying civilization.

Before you know it, tribes that hadn't figured out how to magically grow grains came to raid the store houses of those that did. Hittites battled the Moabites, Hooterites fought the Fuzzites. The nonstop war of the -ites was on.

And if they weren't fighting over grain or goats or women, there was always, "My-God-is- gooder-than-yours." And so emerged another reason to smite them. Now we had the religious wars, too.

.

IMAGINE THAT!

Chapter 4

Before we go any further, think for a minute. What if you didn't think? At all! Not a thought in your silly little head. Nada! Nothing.

We came from that. There was a time when we were close to the baboons. For most of the hunter-gatherer period, we went about our business just staying alive and procreating without this trivial buzzing in our heads: thought.

Over a period of a few thousand years, we went from grunts and *moph* and *tok* to *umphat* and *octad* (Wow! two syllables) and the sounds began to signify, to stand for something.

In all these years, we were learning to use our hands to fashion things, moving from mud and straw pots and vessels to ones that would last longer, baking them in the sun, eventually discovering iron, making tools, finding plants to use for painting walls and rocks. We were also assigning "sounds" to these items.

Sounds evolved into language, which became the beginning glimmerings of thought. As a certain word came to be accepted, for example FROPT maybe meant "fire." When someone uttered FROPT, a person hearing it began

conceptualizing fire, and perhaps visualizing it in his head (hopefully not in his head or he might get hot-headed).

Then, it happened. We began to think, well, not exactly. We started having "thoughts." Strings of words lumped together. They appeared out-of-the blue in our heads. Some anthropologists speculate that when this happened, the person thought they were hearing the voice of God inside their head. Where else would these thoughts be coming from?

This event is so extraordinary and transforming it bears repeating. **Until language showed up (and thought), there was no worry, no guilt, and no concept of lack.**

Will there be food tomorrow? That's a thought. It wasn't possible to have that thought before we could string words together.

We'd go from one day to the next, "knowing" or assuming (at a deep level, since ordinary knowing as we know it, involves thinking) that we'd find food. Or if we didn't, we "knew" that we could survive.

We were in a symbiotic relationship with nature, our food supply. If, after a few days without food we got famished, lo and behold (as if almost miraculously), we'd come upon a fairly fresh (no use-before date) carcass of a raccoon. Perfect!

Didn't Christ say something like, "Look at the flowers in the field, do they look worried?"

In a healthy state, when we are "aligned with nature," we will find what we need. Without looking. And without worrying (for God's sake!)

Back to food for tomorrow. Once we could produce a surplus, which coincided with the ability to think about it, there appeared tomorrow. **Time to worry about what might happen tomorrow.**

The tribal leaders are now doing a great deal of thinking:

What if there isn't enough? We need more; we can't have too much, we need more. Now we have too much. Let's sell it–no let's hide it so no one will find it. Now we have to protect it. What if the [neighboring and now enemy tribe] finds out? Now we need an army to protect it; what if they take it over? Now we need spies.

Most importantly, we need to keep all of this from our own people, so they don't know that we don't know.

We're now firmly in Old Testament territory. It's a time of the Ishtites smiting the Emulites, the Littlebites gobbling up the goodies of the Smitebites. And on and on. It's endless

warfare seemingly for the sake of warfare. Of course, we could always say it was to defend our God, Yahweh. Or on his behalf. Or that they were godless or had the wrong one.

Back to the garden. Give them some knowledge and look where they run with it! When surplus and thought commingled, we have the whole future laid out for us. Abundance became a problem. A seed of wheat that would reverberate down through the centuries

The agricultural revolution stimulated thinking; both thinking and agriculture became catalysts for civilization.

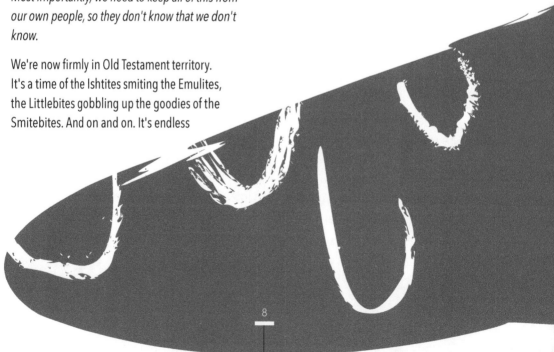

THE GOLDEN AGE

Atlantis

Chapter 5

Did Atlantis exist? If it did, where was it? What happened to it? It was a powerful, advanced island culture that existed over 1200 years before the flowering of the civilization of ancient Greece.

In *The Lost Empire of Atlantis* (Orion, 2011), Gavin Menzies puts forth compelling evidence that Atlantis did exist. He writes it was centered on the island of Crete and was populated by an advanced civilization called the Minoans.

The Minoans were a flourishing empire. They invented coinage, the calendar, a system of standard weights, music, architecture, art and theater. They gave the world exquisite paintings, ceramics and jewelry, and an appreciation of the finer things in life.

The Minoans were also advanced in the knowledge of science, astronomy and engineering. They were skilled at boat building and navigation. Their maritime skills took them to the Upper Peninsula of Michigan where they mined abundant copper, smelt it and brought it back to Atlantis.

They had shown the world that a peaceful existence was a profitable one, embarking on adventures beyond the imagination. They had rulers but they believed in sharing their resources with each other.

Out of that generous impulse, revolutionary ideas such as democracy would evolve.

A volcanic eruption on the nearby island of Thera created a giant tsunami that obliterated Atlantis in 1450 BCE, re-shaping the island.

One thousand years later, the Greek philosopher, Plato, spoke of Atlantis' contributions in the *Timaeus* and in *Critias,* describing the Minoans' many contributions to art and technology in elaborate detail. The Greeks' great works in literature and theater were ostensibly inherited from the Minoans. The Minoans' greatest legacy is the idea of art for art's sake and the pursuit of knowledge for its own intrinsic value. These values were picked up by the Greeks who used them to create a blueprint for their own and for future civilizations.

CLASSICAL

Greek Culture

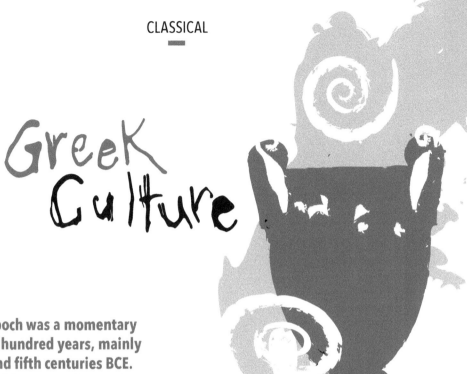

Chapter 6

The Greek epoch was a momentary blip of a few hundred years, mainly the fourth and fifth centuries BCE. It's the period between the Persian wars at the beginning of the fifth century BCE and the death of Alexander the great in 323 BCE. Despite the wars, the Greeks achieved remarkable advances in art and science.

It was an era of unprecedented political and cultural achievements. The Parthenon, Greek tragedy, the historian Herodotus, the philosopher Socrates, the medicinal precepts outlined by Galen and the political reforms of *demokratia* or rule by the people—all established during this time period. They established the foundations for both the Sciences and the Arts that were influential in the following centuries, even up to today.

Though they did have a somewhat ideal government for that time in history, they didn't consider women able to participate in civic life. The Greeks did not have a *demokratia;* then again, no country has achieved it.

Women found an outlet in Dionysius, the God of wine and dance. There were secret initiation rights and rituals that women played a major part in, under the cover of darkness and the influence of wine and other magical substances.

During the Dark Ages, most of the knowledge from the Greek (and Roman) empires was lost (~500 CE – 1300 CE). The Renaissance rediscovered the Greek world, and proceeded to hand it down to the Western World over the next 1000 years.

Imagine we are in Athens in the six century CE, listening to the famous philosopher, Socrates, holding forth in a town Square. He was famous for asking questions of his listeners, forcing them to think and come up with the answer themselves. When asked, "Why do you know so much"? He answered, "I am the only one who knows that he doesn't know anything."

PART TWO

Later History

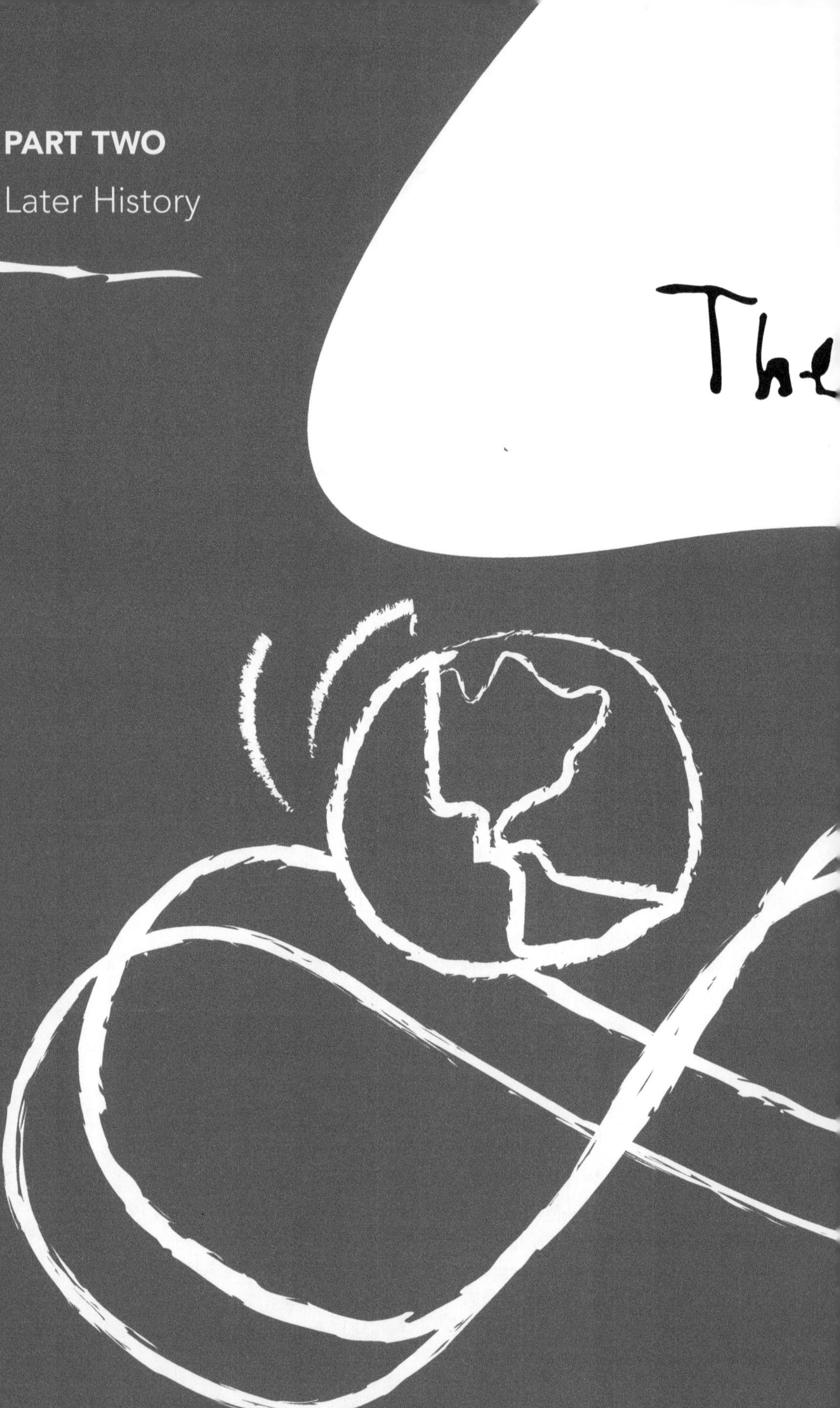

world & patriarchy

Introduction

The world is what we can see and touch, what we experience with our senses. That world has been shaped by men (mostly) who themselves have been molded by patriarchy. We're swimming in a patriarchal ocean. We don't "see" it or "know" it because it envelops us. In a similar way, a fish doesn't "know" or "see" water. We are swimming in the waters of patriarchy.

Patriarchy blankets the planet. There are small pockets of indigenous tribes who haven't come under its spell, who still live as our predecessor hunter-gatherers did, a few million years ago. We can still learn from them what we've lost, while keeping the positive things we've learned.

This section is about the influential role that patriarchy plays in our individual lives as a man or a woman, and also in our collective lives, in the societal and political realms of the world.

Patriarchy

Warps His Story

—

History is at times characterized as *HisStory*. How about *HerStory*? Throughout history, it has been mainly men who wrote the historical records. Naturally they made themselves look good. And up until relatively recent times, women were not accorded a prominent place "at the table." In fact, they prepared the table and then served the "masters." And who would clean up the mess they made?

Patriarchy, the rule of men over women, has played a major role in relations between the sexes. It has also shaped the civilization we have today.

The patriarchal tradition came out of the Old Testament. Surely it was men who concocted the Adam and Eve story which doomed women out of the starting gate.

As that tradition played out through history, men were expected to take advantage of women.

In the following example, I was supposed to "fib a little," and use my position as a man to take advantage of a woman.

On an early, dark, rainy morning, I was navigating my Toyota pickup truck to my day job at a local junior high school. I was approaching a familiar intersection, where a middle-aged Hispanic woman in a sedan was facing me, waiting to turn left across the intersection. When the light turned green for her, she began a slow, deliberate left-hand turn, right in front of me. Despite my being aware that my light had gone from yellow to red, I maintained my speed directly toward her. Even though she now clearly had the right-of-way, I couldn't believe her car kept moving into my lane. She was not following my script (that is, "Stop and wait for me you lowly woman!").

Bam! The rain-slicked street didn't allow me to slow quickly enough. I T-boned the passenger side of her car. We were both in shock. I got out of my pickup, walked around to her car, got into her front seat to get out of the rain, offered an abject, sincere apology. "I'm sorry, it was my fault." Her English was not great. I assured her she didn't have to worry.

Her car was badly damaged but she was able to drive it into the parking lot of a nearby storefront. We exchanged our information. I said I'd inform my insurance company and take care of it. My front end was damaged but I was able to continue on to my job as a teacher.

My insurance company leaned on me to make it her fault, for not stopping. Would it be a lie? Technically, she was supposed to wait until the intersection was clear before she proceeded. Instead of admitting fault, I could make it her fault. I actually wrestled with it: my inner knowing of the truth (and what I had admitted to her) and the outer "truth of the patriarchal world," i.e., what they wanted me to do/say.

When this happened, I was 45 years old. My moral compass was pointing in the right direction, but not yet fully focused. The insurance company's bait sought to sow doubt on my initial feelings at the time of impact. Had I gone along with their script, I would have set myself up to bend the truth next time. Not good for me, nor humanity. I would also have had to endure the pain of lying to that woman's poor face.

Patriarchy foisted this moral dilemma on me.

The male priorities of power and control have tilted us off center. The result is what we see in today's world, a world characterized by greed, competition, and violence. It is a world out of balance.

Human beings "out of balance" create an earth out of balance. Most of the soil of the earth has been so stressed and stretched that nothing will grow on it without the aid of added inoculations.

The masculine version of history represents a story we could title:

Let's see what we can get away with, how far we can go using our collective minds and willpower.

The forces at play in this scenario are working against nature, seeing it as something to be used, not respected as sacred, as part of the life chain. People themselves are also seen as subjects to be utilized.

The tycoons who run the world have managed to foist the ideas of profit and competition onto the general populous, making it appear as though that's the only way to make a living.

THE Good News

Short-lived for Women

Chapter 8

In the New Testament, Christ brought the "Good News." Women felt particularly benefitted by the "Good News." What they heard in his message was they would no longer be tethered to the yokes of men if they took his words to heart. He didn't differentiate between men and women. One of his most faithful followers was a woman of ill repute, Mary Magdalene.

In the days after Christ's Resurrection, when the Good News was spreading like wildfire, women were at the forefront. They were actively, enthusiastically, and joyfully spreading the tenets of New Life that Christ had brought. It looked like the start of Herstory.

But men were not on board for the feminine vessel that was ferrying the Good News. And, to continue this allegory, they decided to sink it. The Good News was about freeing humans from the bondage of the world and from the suffering brought by being bound to it. That meant women were freed from the bondage of patriarchy which was enmeshed with the world. **But patriarchy pushed back.**

The early Church Fathers, (patriarchs!), began formalizing the "Church" services. Initially there was a loose structure of meetings being held in people's homes in various cities, as evidenced in the epistles of Saint Paul. Women played an important role in these meetings.

Next thing you know, the communal church table has male priests, bishops and archbishops and even a stand-in for Christ—a pope. It has a legacy story of male disciples who were singularly responsible for spreading the word. And the women? Well, they were not exactly invited to that same table, the one they were more than ready to serve.

But women managed to maintain a powerful presence in the early centuries. They continued to do so, albeit almost underground, through the medieval period and into the modern era. They nursed the flickering flame of the spiritual realm, while continuing to butt up against men's strictures.

Once Christ let the genie out of the bottle, however, it could never be put back inside, despite the best efforts of men. Women never forgot the ecstatic rush they felt in those post-Resurrection years. It's embedded in women today as they continue to bend back the bars of patriarchy.

THE

Yin Yang

Chapter 9

In Chinese thought, Yin is the feminine, Yang the masculine. Every human being has both these aspects within themselves.

A man's character will display a preponderance of Yang offset by some Yin. The opposite is also possible, and everything in between. But within that individual, the Yin and Yang will be in balance, if his body and spirit is healthy. If he's been allowed and/or encouraged to express both aspects of himself, he will be in harmony, in balance with himself and with the outer world/universe. The balance can change day to day (even hour by hour), as situations may call for one or the other as needed. For example, if someone challenges me, I may "decide" my Yin will be a more effective strategy than my Yang. Or it might be the opposite.

Patriarchy, which denigrates the "feminine attributes," makes it more difficult for men to "own" their Yin. Herein lies most of the ills of humanity,

hence the reason for this book. Patriarchy, as a sociological construct, suppresses the natural balance of Yin and Yang in men.

The same ratio balance applies to women. Mostly Yin, some Yang, with all the various combinations that make life fascinating and beautiful. Imagine how boring it would be if every woman had the same amount of Yin! Men would yank!

Western culture, and increasingly Eastern as well, values Yang more than Yin.

It's a Yang world after all. People are essentially off balance.

But we're so accustomed to imbalance that it escapes our notice.

I suspect I am about as much Yin as Yang. I've always preferred the company of women over men, of kids and babies over adults. I've had guys show interest in me but I'm not wired to reciprocate.

As I've gotten older, I am more able to accept and appreciate my gentleness, empathy, and tears. But as a teenager, I had to hide my Yin side and pretend to be "one of the boys." I was fearless with no emotions. The story of my life has been a seesaw between the Yin and Yang within me, and my ability/ inability to understand them and to express them in a world that doesn't welcome balance.

& horizontal

Vertical

Chapter 10

Christ on the cross. The archetype. A perfect representation of the infinite vertical dimension and the finite horizontal dimension (Eckhart Tolle).

The vertical board/beam connecting the earth to the heavens represents the spiritual dimension. The horizontal beam represents the day-to-day earthly plane of existence. Our current reality: get out of bed each morning, still tired, going to work/school/office, deal with surly people in traffic—all the stuff that comes up in our everyday life story.

Whether we know it or not, we interact with life on both the vertical and horizontal planes. The stories and narratives that embody human history are made up of events from the intersection of these two planes. Every day we are challenged to choose how much of each dimension we embody in our life story.

I've always thought of myself as a good person and I made it a goal. It was the early 1970s. When I was a young, married adult with adolescent-age children of my own, I was teaching at a high school. One day, one of my students missed the bus so I found myself driving her home. In a shocking revelation, she confided to me that her adoptive dad was sexually abusing her. While she was revealing this intimate confession of abuse, I was further shocked to realize there was a part of me that wanted to abuse her. To make matters worse, in those days, I was powerless to do anything for her. I remained silent. So much for my goal to be a good person.

That's a difficult confession to make, even now. It seems so horrible, cruel, and cold. At that moment, in the car, the horizontal and vertical planes intersected. The patriarchal influence (horizontal) was at war with my moral compass of right and wrong (vertical).

The horizontal plane can be likened to the world of form. It is also an expression of the mind that's attuned to the world's dark resonant frequencies. It's definitely amplified by patriarchy.

The vertical dimension is the spirit, the spiritual element of our human existence. It gets blocked out by the machinations of our crazy world, but it still lives within us. It links to our *Inner Body*, animating our *Awareness* and fueling our *Presence*. It is that aspect of ourselves that's always ready to be accessed, to be lived, to be listened to. It is timeless, unchanging.

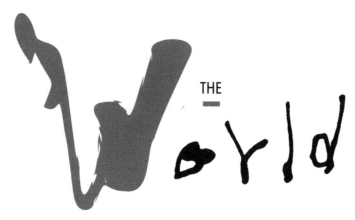

THE World

Built to Patriarchal Specs

Chapter 11

We are born into a beautiful, warm, magical world with wondrous, loving creatures hovering over us, bestowing joyous energy and sensuous touch. That's our first world experience. We pass through a childhood world with other kids and adults, some bigger, some nice, some mean. The adolescent world presents us with new learning opportunities, with challenging physical and psychological changes, followed by our inevitable adulthood that expresses even more profound changes as we wrestle with work, independence, and new relationships.

There are the contrasting "worlds" of civilization versus nature. Nature, whether a small park in the midst of a bustling city or a vast national park, provides a sharp, welcome contrast to the busy buildings and the rapid, mechanized pace that colors a city.

The "world" includes all of this, everything we see and interact with on a daily basis. That world, with all its marvels and problems, is the one we have created.

It was our forebears that hammered the nails, laid the concrete, built the roads, schools and stores to sell goods and services.

Workers are busy now, continuing to build according to the "patriarchal framework" that's been established. That framework includes a belief system that encompasses competition, greed, and scarcity. The latter makes competition a positive value.

And once you're thinking "scarcity," you will always want more and more, and never feel you have enough.

The corporation is a product of patriarchy. It's usually a hierarchical model, stressing competition. The goal is money and power.

Let's look at XYZ Corporation as a hypothetical example. It's a company specializing in helping farmers to fix their "spoiled soil."

The X division markets a product called, Soil Helpers, to farmers to enable them to increase the yield of their crops. The Y division is set up to handle the lawsuits expected since Soil Helpers contains numerous toxic chemicals, some possible cancer-causing carcinogens. The Z division is busy building the indoor farming towers (an invention that requires no soil) that will be needed once Soil Helpers depletes the earth's soil beyond redemption.

There's also a public relations campaign exposing "cloud change" as the reason why farmers' soil continues to deteriorate, despite lavish treatments of Soil Helpers. According to their "scientific report":

Cloud change is reported to be the reason for the dead soil, soil that has lost the ability to persuade a plant to poke its head out of the ground. Cloud change is brought on by flatulence, not just of cows as formerly thought, but also of human beings. All of these make their way into the clouds and when it rains, look out below!

Fortunately, a pharmaceutical company discovered a pill, STOPFT! For people to take which controls the flatulence. Unfortunately, one of the side effects is they belch a lot and the gasses are not pleasant.

Another pill, Sweetenda, gives the belched gas a sweet taste and also makes it "cloud resistant."

In the previous, hypothetical example, the solution to the problem (the farmer's yields diminishing), is assumed to come from outside sources. Nature herself is deficient; she needs help, man-made additives.

This assumption is part of the patriarchal blueprint, that men are in charge of nature and may have to tweak it or even twist it, in order to persuade it to do his bidding. Nature's not enough..

The same applies to human nature. We are thought to be "not quite enough," perhaps contaminated by "sin," or maybe our nature is naturally lacking and needs outside help to govern it and to keep it healthy.

These are taken-for-granted beliefs of the world that we grew up with, that we inhabit now, and they underlie the ways in which we approach the world.

But we don't need to subscribe to patriarchy nor to its underlying beliefs. As Christ pointed out when someone was worried about having enough to eat, "look at the Lillies of the field; are they concerned about tomorrow?"

What is missing from the patriarchal perspective is believing in human nature, and in the abundance of nature.

Humans are now waking up to how incredibly powerful our own bodies are in keeping us healthy, if only we give them the respect and care they deserve.

Missing from the "world picture," is the hidden, *Invisible World* beneath the one we see with our eyes. This is the essential "World" that each of us has within us, the one we can *touch* at any moment simply by being *still*. In a moment of non-thinking stillness, we can at once put in proper perspective the outer, problematic, fragmented world that we see and the *Inner World* that is perfect, never-changing.

When we realize this dimension, we're able to "wake up" from the dream-like slumber we've been in, the one fostered by patriarchy, with its self-limiting beliefs towards ourselves, and its nature-ravaging perspective.

We are moving into a new world, one in which women will find themselves able to once again exert their magic.

propaganda

Promotes Patriarchy

Chapter 12

My story starts with my gender, I'm male.

This fact has the biggest impact on the trajectory of my story. If I had been born female, I likely would have experienced a totally different outcome.

Male or female, that's a key element of our story because we live in a patriarchal world. It's a skewed world, one out-of-balance. It is built on the lie that men are superior to women. Though we can no longer say this publicly, it is a bed-rock belief that's been handed down for about 10,000 years.

Women are inferior.

Patriarchy received its foundational blessing in the genesis story when Eve tempted Adam to take a bite of the apple. She gets blamed for getting all of us (her progeny) kicked out of the garden. The trick worked. Adam takes over and men are the victors, women the victims.

This belief becomes doctrine. The Roman Catholic Church teaches this "propaganda," and it seeps into the heads and hearts of men and women and remains for thousands of years, till it becomes "normal."

Patriarchy has been a disaster for thousands of years, not just for women, but men too. Not to mention civilization, which is now on the brink of self-destruction. Its longevity and "success," is due to propaganda. Propaganda is the act of trying to influence another person to believe or join their cause or program. Here's an example: an anti-gun group wants me to turn in my BB gun and join their group. They provide "information" on why it's a good idea. The clincher is they will give me a free squirt gun if I join them.

That's propaganda, advertising. It's no wonder the word, propaganda, is so close to the word, propagation. That is its entire motive, to propagate what needs to be spread out of self-interest.

No propaganda is needed to influence boys to join the "patriarchal club." They're automatically enrolled at birth. But they're given a few years to "roam free." Then, at the first sign of "soft, feminine emotions," they are ridiculed into capitulation. Join the patriarchy or suffer.

Groomed to continue the tradition. A secret society.

This is part of being a man—a rite of passage. If the young man has an older brother, he may "box his ears," roughing him up a bit so that he can "hold his own" and fight like a man.

The propaganda that underpins patriarchy is conveyed person to person—in the family, by our peers, and in organizations we belong to. It's demonstrated by boys' behavior towards each other and towards girls. It culminates in puberty

and adolescence, a difficult period made more so by the insecurities and befuddlement of that age. It is present in social media's depiction of male and female behaviors, their looks and body image. It's in music, movies, news, the ads and commercials on TV, the Internet and billboards.

The Roman Catholic Church and Propaganda

In 1622, Pope Gregory the XV set up a committee of cardinals of the Roman Catholic Church. They would be responsible for foreign missions, the *congregatio de propaganda fide* (congregation for propagation of faith).

Just ten years later, a Jesuit, Paul Le Jeune, was Superior of the French Mission at Quebec. He wintered with the Montagnais–Naskapi Indians. He was horrified at what he saw: indulgent parents, independent women, "divorced" men and women, men with two wives, and no formal leaders. It was a peripatetic, relaxed culture in which women enjoyed a high economic and social status. (*Women: Down through The Ages, How Lies Have Shaped Our Lives*, Schaefer, republished 2023).

This native culture stood patriarchy on its head. Its way of life was antithetical, not just to patriarchy, but to the church as well. The missionaries' role, functioning as emissaries of the church (and indirectly the government) was to bring them into the church's fold, and to fold them into the government's control. He taught them lifetime monogamy, male authority, and female obedience. Ten years later, men in the tribe began beating their wives (*Anatomy of Love*, Fisher, 1994).

The missionaries were also hard at work on the native population in New England. The evangelists' biggest challenge was convincing the wives to reform their husbands into becoming masters over them. Wife beating was not mentioned as a side effect.

The missionaries' worldview and belief system were a reflection of the propaganda they had received. It made it impossible for them to appreciate the natives' sacred views of life and nature. The beauty and harmony of the family seemed ugly and profane to them.

Patriarchal Propaganda and Our Stories

Patriarchy underpins our individual stories. Its core beliefs of competition and struggle lead to an increased atomization of life. We become separate from one another, less reliant on "clan life" or community-based living. We're separated when we travel (relying on small, individual travel vehicles), in our work (more reliant on interfacing with gadgets, computerized modeling, and artificial intelligence), in our healthcare (artificial treatments replacing

nature's natural cures), and in our food consumption (most of our food is processed with zero nutrition).

The "Patriarchal Program" has made our lives more artificial, taken us farther and farther away from nature. Men, influenced by patriarchy, see nature as something to be conquered for profit. Whatever course men decide to take (even if it means the desecration of land and negative, toxic effects for people) there will be justification (propaganda) to make it seem right and even necessary.

Women on the other hand, tend to identify with nature and respect it. They usually see the larger picture, but that's not the one that patriarchy has in mind. Their input has not been sought.

Humans

Hitched to Robots

—

Chapter 13

Welcome to life 3.0 (a.k.a. the Fourth Industrial Revolution, the Bio Industrial Convergence). This is the next phase of our evolution. It's time to graduate into the world of artificial intelligence, a world wherein we will gradually merge into a new life form. The new humans will be smarter, stronger, and their lifespan will not be subject to the usual limitations.

Trans-humanism will bring about a new life form on the planet, created by humans, that will become symbiotic with humans without the usual limitations.

Social robots will interact with humans. We'll have a direct interface with artificial intelligence. Whatever the problem, we'll have the immediate answer.

Humans are already becoming more like machines. We get injections (vaccines) to update our software (immune system). And machines are becoming more and more like humans. We can chat with them on the internet and phone as they pretend to care about us and help us solve our problems.

Humans, like computers, get a bug and need an upgrade to take care of it. They can simply check their "dashboard" to see the status of their various systems/symptoms. They'll see whether they need a new vaccine, whether it's for a viral bug or perhaps a "personality" bug."

The above is not a far-fetched science fantasy. It's here. At least in the minds of an elite group of crazed technocrats who are intent on foisting this new "scientific" vision on humanity. Science according to them is what they say it is. One of their famous lines is: "You will own nothing and be happy." But will people actually go for it? They go on to say, "Fear of death and germaphobia will drive people into the arms of our fold." Don't get trapped by these fears.

This is what thought has wrought.

They believe that their thoughts are real, and their actions are geared towards carrying out plans for humanity based on faulty assumptions (thoughts/ ideas). Hijacked by their thoughts... and in order to achieve their objectives, they're willing to suspend common sense, do the unthinkable.

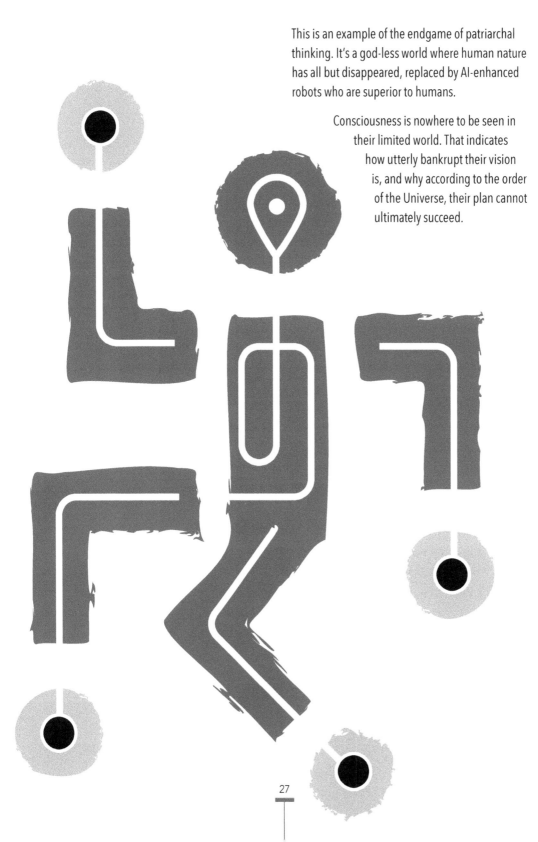

This is an example of the endgame of patriarchal thinking. It's a god-less world where human nature has all but disappeared, replaced by AI-enhanced robots who are superior to humans.

Consciousness is nowhere to be seen in their limited world. That indicates how utterly bankrupt their vision is, and why according to the order of the Universe, their plan cannot ultimately succeed.

Ego

Chapter 14

Animals do not have egos. They are not concerned with how they look or if they fit in. More importantly, they don't judge. The reason you love your dog so much is because when you look into his eyes, he looks right back at you–no filters, no judgement. You see your pure self in the dog.

In the same breath, a mass-murderer can come home after a "fulfilling" day's work of mayhem and destruction of peoples' lives, and his dog will welcome him with an unreserved shower of love, licking the hand that handled the knife. This is one of the weird facts of life. If we find ourselves sitting in judgment over that, that's our ego taking over.

The patriarchal mindset is fertile ground for the ego to grow and thrive. Patriarchy and ego share some fundamental ideas: they both crave competition, hierarchy, and conflict. For example, the patriarchal idea that men are superior to women fits perfectly with the ego's natural tendency to compete with and to judge others.

On the business level, the patriarchal ideas of competition and power-seeking equate perfectly with the ego's tendency to keep women's job status and salary below that of a man. Accordingly, men set up barriers to keep women out of the "Club" (men only). This is the ego/mind devising strategies to differentiate and separate women.

In the "bedroom world", as in the business world, men like to "lord" it over women. In the sexual realm, the minds of men are sometimes completely overtaken by the egoic thinking mind, veering off into dangerous, oppressive fantasies towards the female sex.

Our egos have a natural tendency to judge other people–the way they walk, talk, dress–usually unfavorably in comparison to ourselves. If we're *thinking* when we're around people, we're most likely judging them. **In this way our ego and our thinking mind are linked together.**

Our ego is interested in its own survival. It wants to preserve the only thing it knows: our past story. It desires to maintain it in order to keep intact our image, "the way another person sees us." And it wants us to focus on the future, which doesn't exist. Anything but the present!

Since it wants to maintain us the way we are, it's totally opposed to "being in the moment," which is unpredictable. It's also where/when we're most alive. We are *human beings*. Ego only cares about the *human* part, the horizontal plane of our existence. It knows nothing of *Being*, the vertical plane.

In other words, we become identified with our thoughts about it completely. We cannot see ourselves outside this identity. This is the ego activated in its full form. It might be a political party or a religious group—or a particular belief that one of these groups espouses. We are constantly being asked to "join" their cause, to believe in it. Our ego loves to join the fray, to do battle on the side of righteousness. The ego needs an enemy, someone to be wrong.

Thinking can be useful when solving problems, creating art, and inventing things. It becomes highly problematic when we believe a certain idea or a line of thinking is who we are.

Consciousness

Evolution and Suffering

—

Chapter 15

The ultimate story, the real story behind the story, is consciousness. Consciousness is the goal of humanity. We are here to become conscious. Once we become aware of that, our experience of daily life changes.

We are evolving to a new rung on the ladder of consciousness. The ladder reaches to the stars. Our goal is not to reach the stars, but to enjoy each rung and to participate fully in it.

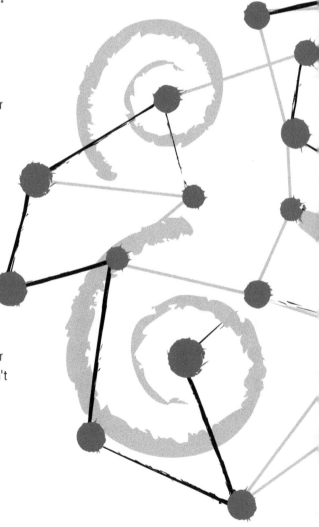

During our unconscious sleep time, we process the day's data – all of our thoughts, emotions, experiences – adding them to our inventory. As we awaken in the morning, it might not dawn on us that we're different. Sometimes it's subtle and we may not notice it. Other times, Boom! We decide to move to Timbuktu.

The difference shows up in our daily interactions. We might greet the store clerk with more feeling or notice something different about her/him we hadn't noticed the day before. Our relationship with our spouse, our kids, our dog/cat are all evolving, day-to-day. That evolution involves suffering.

Suffering is part of the experience of being alive. Most of it is non-physical. If I break my leg, there will be some pain, but most of my suffering will

enabled
enabled

be my reaction to it, what I make of it (thinking about the past–how wonderful to dance) and the future (how my lifestyle will be crippled). These are all thoughts and not related to the injury itself. If we could experience injury without thinking, we would suffer much less.

However, if suffering is to benefit us, we do need to accept it, and not complain about the unfairness of it all.

If we resist suffering, we are resisting change/ growth, resisting what life wants to teach us.

While we're evolving on an individual level, mankind as a whole is doing it on a collective scale. This is necessary at this time because mankind is approaching a precipice. The forces leading us to the precipice are threatening our lives and livelihood.

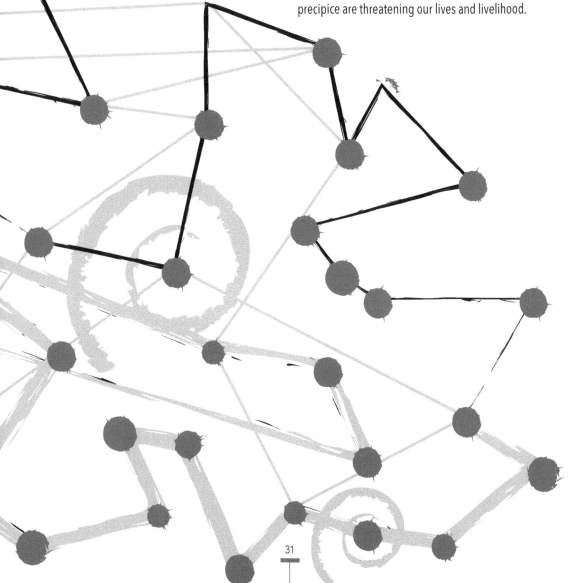

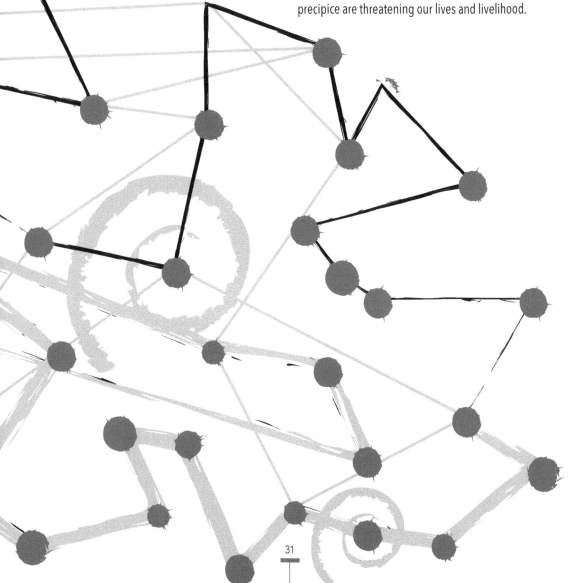

PART THREE
Female and Male

THE

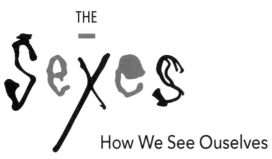

How We See Ouselves

The task of the 21st-century is to restore the grandeur of women, so that they can once again take their rightful place at the absolute center of life.

Men, unshackled from the castrating beliefs of patriarchy—basically that men are not just superior to women, but that women are somehow defective (not quite fully human) –will be able to admit their vulnerabilities, even admit being jealous of women's assets

Breasts are just the tip of the iceberg.

Sex has been hijacked to service the marketplace. The marketplace is an offshoot/side effect of some of the viral influences of patriarchy: competition/greed/ violence.

Introduction

In prehistoric civilizations, women played an outsized part, as evidenced in the artistic representations that have been unearthed. At times their breasts are enlarged to grotesque proportions, and as often, it's their belly that balloons out.

Clearly, women were admired, even worshipped, for their magical ability to produce babies from their own flesh and to accompany this astounding feat with the almost-as-grand-trick of suckling the newly hatched baby at her breast to keep it alive.

Once "civilization" got underway, women were tossed under the plow of agriculture, their fate sealed by the stamp of patriarchy.

In the 21st-century, the patriarchal "run of history" is reaching its climax. It has had some successes, but it's no longer playing well at the box office.

Men have been encumbered and handicapped throughout history by having to pretend that they could manage the daily tasks of setting up a society and governing a state without women. Yes it's possible, but it's not pretty.

THE STORY OF

Women

Chapter 16

Women are the primal mother creatures. We speak of Mother Earth. Women also share a kinship with the moon, synchronizing their menstrual cycles with that of the moon.

The glorious magnificence of their physical bodies defies words. Prehistoric peoples, enthralled by their natural beauty and their seeming magical power to produce new life, left behind countless metal and stone replicas of women. Later, the beauty of one particular woman, Helen of Troy, caused the Greeks and the Trojans to battle each other in a long, drawn out, senseless war. Years later, it would be the ravishing charms of Cleopatra that brought Egypt into battle with Rome. A few millennia later, *West Side Story* featured Maria at the center of a conflict between rival gangs.

What is it that men are fighting for? Do they sense something is missing? Perhaps a lack, something that needs filling?

Michelangelo, Picasso, Reubens, Dante and many others have tried to capture in portraits, stone and words the ravishing beauty of women.

In a word, women are simply stunning. Men are stunned.

And that's just on the physical realm of form. A woman also has, as every life form does, that which is not visible, but which sustains and is necessary for the very existence of life itself. She has her life force, spirit or soul, the source of her vitality and energy.

It is her hidden essence that also renders her attractive. Even irresistible. And the combination? Mine blowing, mind shattering! It's no wonder–let's admit it–they scare the bejesus out of us.

In our DNA, there is the double helix, a spinning spiral of opposing strains of nucleic acid that mirror each other and provide a program for our body to carry out.

We might visualize women and men relating to each other in a double helix. If it were magnetized, it would be the female half of the magnetic strain that would be providing the attractive force.

The male would be along for the ride. He would be responding to her charge. Willingly, pleasurably, even ecstatically. It could be the dance of life itself.

Female babies are born with immense potential. But they are not accorded the respect and reverence of their pre-patriarchal sisters. Like Prometheus, women keep pushing the rock up the hill, only to find it roll back down, nullifying their progress. Men are now realizing that it's not just hurting women to keep making the hill steeper, the stone heavier.

There should be no hill, no struggle.

THE STORY OF

—

Chapter 17

Men are men are men are men. What are men? What is a man?

There's no easy answer. Men are typically bigger and stronger than women, so one of our roles has been to protect women. Formerly from wild and dangerous animals, today from wild and dangerous men (who are animals).

We have defined ourselves in relation to women as opposite. Women are hot, men are cold. Men are rational, women are irrational. Men are opposed to women because they are opposite. Women have become the default definition of what a man is not. If a woman is "this," a man is not that (this).

In this discussion (and throughout the book), we are using male and female in simple, traditional terms, which includes stereotyping. It is beyond the scope of this book to include the various nuances/gradations of the sexes with the accompanying pronouns and adjectives that have become common of late.

Men go out of their way to not act or look feminine. Women tend to be dainty. A woman will carefully sip tomato soup from a small

spoon as she sits upright in her starched blouse and kerchief. A man sitting next to her will lift the bowl to his mouth with both hands and loudly slurp the soup into his mouth, using his sleeve to wipe away some of the red soup that slid onto his beard.

If they resemble two distinct species, that's no accident. Be a Man! Man-up! Act like a man!

There's no shortage of exhortations about "Being a Man." But it's hard to know what is meant by this. Is there a taken-for-granted-shared-understanding or agreement of what a man is?

If there were,

it might be something like this: a man is anything but a woman.

A woman is emotional, easily displaying her feelings. A man doesn't have feelings or doesn't display them if he does.

A "real man" is the Marine in a recruitment poster. With a stiff, reserved face that would shatter in pieces if he were to break a smile. Or in the old westerns, John Wayne is the ideal man: always serious, gruff in manner, not a playful bone in his bony, chiseled face.

There seems to be a shared idea of what masculinity means. It came out of Patriarchy around 10,000 years ago, and it's still operative today.

When I entered St. Margaret School as a 1st grader, I was terrified. I wanted to be part of my desk, nothing else. By the 4th or 5th grades, I had made some friends and they decided (I'm guessing) that I needed a little "manly" training.

One morning I was in the boys' bathroom with them when Freddy Watkins walked in. Freddy was pudgy, had a fat stomach. My friends told me to hit him, to punch him.

I couldn't believe the words I heard! They made no sense whatsoever! Why hit him? I didn't know him, had never talked to him. But they were serious. And Insistent: GO Ahead, Sock him in the stomach, HIT Him!

With difficulty, I reluctantly forced my hesitant fist to hit his protruding stomach, and immediately withdrew it. His stomach wasn't as soft as it looked.

Freddy started to cry. I looked at him dumfounded. My handlers seemed pleased that I had showed some manhood. I was as confused as ever.

We can't understand what we are as men without understanding patriarchy.

Patriarchy was set up as a framework for men to run amuck. That's the simple truth. In the beginning, men owned women outright, they were his property. Women had no rights. Early Israelite law stated if a man was killed in battle, his wife would go to the man who killed her husband.

Patriarchy today is quite different. But there's still some remnants: "Boys will be boys," means males can still be expected to "run amuck," and maybe "spread a little seed here and there."

Despite the freedoms that have been afforded women in the last four hundred years, they still

must be careful after dark. Men are still regarded as predators, untrustworthy.

For men who have bought into patriarchy as their bible, the battlefields of killing and rape become natural extensions of their self-definition. Fighting, war and violence are the proving ground for manhood. Rape an accepted/expected perk.

Throughout my life, I've been confused about my masculine identity, uncomfortable with the lie I felt forced to maintain.

I felt unsure of myself around girls. What did they want? What was I supposed to want? On a date, I knew I was supposed to try to "make out" and see "how far I could get." How crazy is that?!

If a *How-to-Deal-With-Men* manual were written for women, it might say: "When dealing with the male species, it is important to remember they have been indoctrinated for thousands of years with strange ideas about women. They believe they have a right to ask for 'our favors' and that we're under some sort of 'understood obligation' to comply. Just say NO! Otherwise, they'll never learn."

Men have to pretend they're something they are not. They are not rugged, angry-looking cowboys. They are not lone individuals here to save the world. They're simply human beings who desire to be human, but are given the wrong script.

I remember walking home with my little brother after watching an afternoon matinee at the local theater.

I felt like the cowboy hero in the movie, ready to conquer the world. Halfway home, a boy challenged me. This should be easy, I thought. It was over in one or two punches, my nose bloodied. I'd been knocked off my imaginary throne.

Patriarchy is a lie. But it still informs our notion of what it is to be a man. Which means that "Being Male" involves pretending. Putting on an act.

That means we basically don't own our sexual selves, don't own our masculinity. How can we own up to it?

It's time to change the script, re-write the story, trash the patriarch narrative. Fill in the feminine parts (and allow women to actually be feminine!). It's already happening. But we can speed it along. Shed light on it. Light dispels darkness. The truth deserves to shine. Both men and women deserve to find the joy that's been covered over by fear.

Patriarchy Promotes Problems

Chapter 18

Men and women are designed to complement (and compliment) each other. It's beautiful to see the built-in complementary parts that fit together like an interlocking puzzle. The design is exquisite!

But what if the design is flawed?

If men are not "at home" in their sexuality, if they're a little shaky about their identity to begin with, it doesn't bode well for how they are going to relate to women.

They will naturally try to compensate for any lack they feel, to make up for this deep-seated lack of confidence (which they may not even be aware of).

They'll display an outward swagger, and try to impress her with their confidence, their abilities and/or accomplishments.

The woman may pretend to be interested in this, but she really wants to know him. What's he really like? Inside?

We're off to a shaky start with the guy not wanting to feel vulnerable. The usual behavioral response is less than desirable...The problem is further complicated by the false flag of equality. Equality is a concept which shouldn't be applied to men and women. It's a divisive concept, meant to distract from the real substantive question: are guys able to laugh and play like little kids?

Equality leads to competition:

who is better at what? It's a wholly unnecessary distraction. Women and men are different. Period.

We need to get back to the kid model. Little kids, if not yet influenced by the media, will not be comparing whether boys or girls are better. At my grade school, Lynn Warner was the fastest runner. No boy could beat her. End of story. When I was in the first grade, Bobbi Pendergras ruled. No boy would mess with her. That was just accepted.

A major factor in men/women relationships is the mindset. What are the *expectations?* Expectations involve the mind. When the mind comes into play, it brings up its constant companion: *thinking.*

Here things get tricky. If both parties in a relationship are normal, meaning they are thinking all the time, their relationship will not get beyond the brief puppy love stage followed by the much longer: "How-can-I-possibly-have-ever-imagined-spending-the-rest-of-my-life-with-this-jerk?"

Where is the exit sign?

Thinking puts us in a different time zone. We're either thinking about how great the first date was, or wondering what she/he will say tomorrow to upset us.

We need to be present, each for the other, otherwise we're simply "ships passing in the night." There's no recognition. When we're *present*, and not in a thinking state, we are able to *see* each other, not just as humans, but as human *Beings.*

Once we become aware of that, it's possible to move beyond the humdrum level of problem-filled relationships.

Masculinity

Chapter 19

Men are being prodded by our "sisters" to explore what it is to be a man. This is new stuff, uncharted territory. We haven't really tried it out.

On a recent zoom call on spirituality that was focused on this topic, the women were insisting that we "call it out" when you hear guys getting into their locker room banter.

One of the guys replied that, if he did that, he'd get an argumentative response and maybe not get invited to the next golf outing. But, he went on, if I brought up how wonderful my wife is, the tone of the conversation changed: They weren't going to dispute my experience with my wife.

That same guy told of an experience he had with a woman that he was seeing on zoom conference calls, dealing with spirituality. What started out as a spiritually driven conversation, gradually went in a different direction. Both parties sensed an attraction to the other.

She sent some videos for him to look at that were tantalizing, a bit racy. She asked if he wanted to see more.

Here lies the trap, the question everyone faces in one shape or another, at some moment in time: yay, or nay? In response, he said he was reluctant to go further, though he could feel a part of himself (probably his ego), was more than willing. Familiar sexual fantasies surfaced, but when he let them subside, he became aware of the deep peace and pleasure he felt from remaining in a balanced relationship with himself, his family and Being Itself..

This is a new paradigm shift for men.

That's what we need in order to gain respect for ourselves, and it's long overdue for our lovely sisters.

THE PROBLEM WITH

Breasts

Chapter 20

Women have them.

Men don't.

**They're
incredibly beautiful,
tantalizing
and attractive.**

Men still don't.

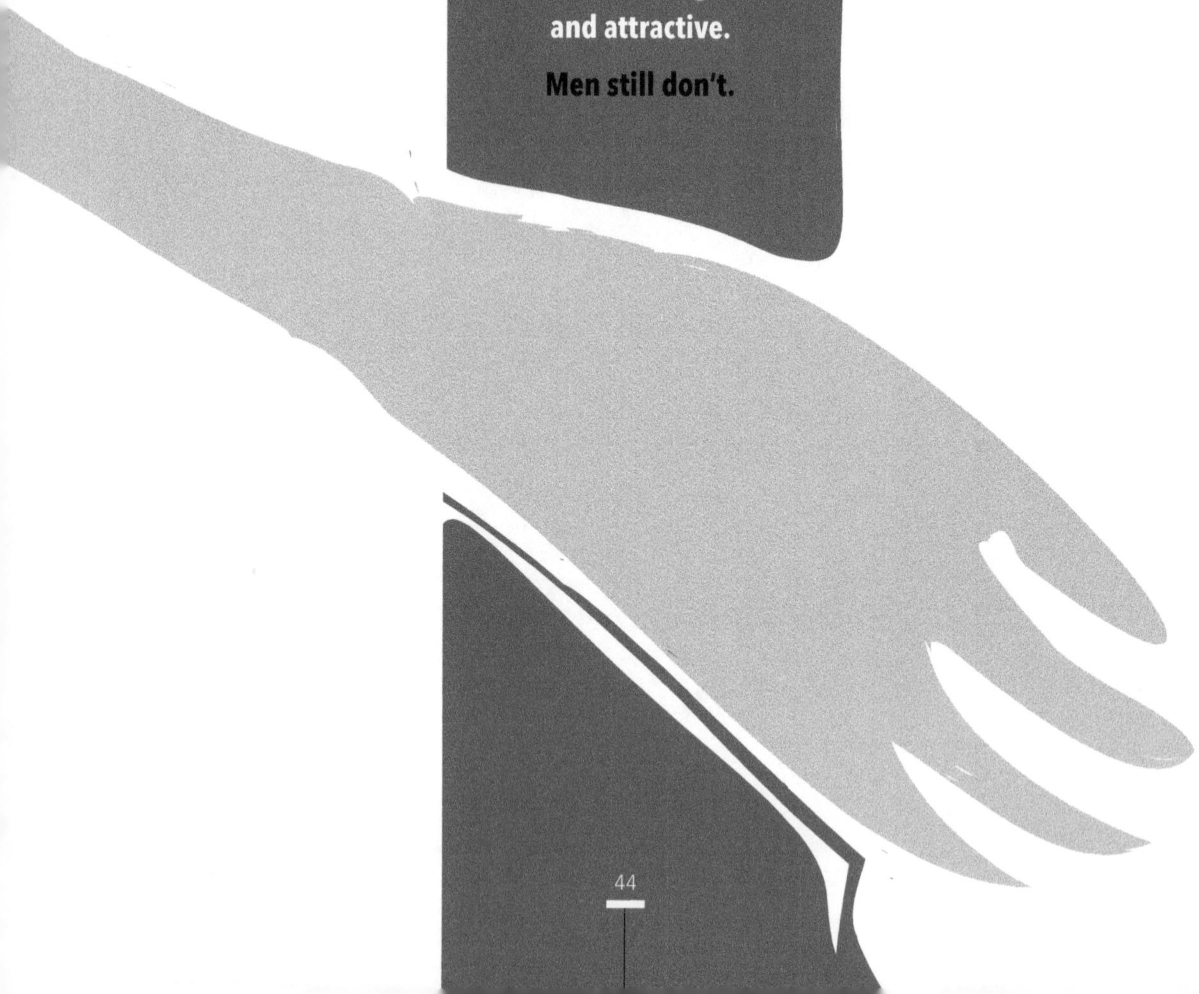

A PERSONAL

Odyssey

Chapter 21

Not far into my second marriage, my wife and I were dancing at a local night club. My wife noticed that I was looking at other women on the dance floor.

"Why are you looking at them instead of me?" I didn't know what to say. How did she know?

Once she noticed it, it became even more noticeable to me. It was now a "thing," something that I was doing. Despite my efforts to hide it—to pretend I was surveying the walls of the room or the lighting on the ceiling as I glanced around—it didn't work.

I wasn't fooling anyone.

Stopping it didn't appear on the horizon of possibility.

Now that she was aware of this proclivity, it suddenly became a problem for me whenever we were around other women. It started to bother me that I gaped at other women. I didn't want to cause trouble, or have it become another issue in our marriage.

When away from her, I was able to indulge freely. And I did.

While attending classes at California State University Dominguez Hills, attractive women overwhelmed my ocular circuits. Way too many beautiful breasts to sort out. My perceptions were on overload.

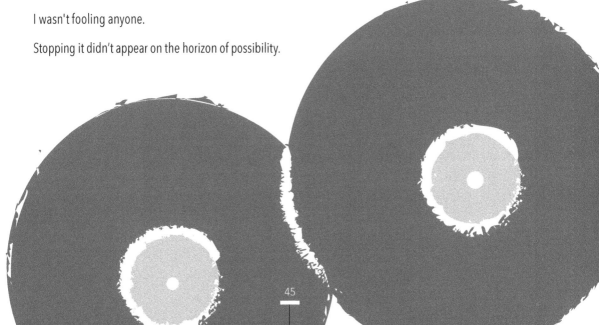

Just walking around on campus, going from one place to another or from one building to another, my eyes assessed an abundance of attraction. It proved to be too much.

One Monday afternoon during lunch break, I sat on the grass and noticed a group of young coeds, maybe five or six, standing a little ways away, in animated conversation. Punctuated by short bursts of laughter. My attention riveted on them. I didn't stare, but I continually surveyed them as I glanced around, then came back to them. Each one had a particular attraction. I was mesmerized. Time stopped.

More than mesmerized, I was hooked.

It dawned on me at that moment that I could not stop looking, even if I wanted to. I did try. I looked away, tried to think of something else. But back my eyes went. I'd look away, only to find my eyes drawn back. Again and again.

I was jealous that women had these divinely designed orbs of flesh that magnetically locked onto a man's attention grid and stopped him in his tracks.

I realized my addiction had become a serious problem, a behavior I could not control. In the classroom, I'd be looking around at women instead of listening to the lecture. If my special education classes were not so easy, I never would have passed and got my teaching credential. I realized I needed to do something about it. Now that I had admitted to myself the reality, I noticed even more how big the problem was.

They were everywhere! I couldn't get away from them. They seemed to be more noticeable than ever. And not just on women that I'd encounter, but on billboards, on TV, in movies, fashion magazines, any magazines–breasts were everywhere, taking over the planet.

I had to act. Do something, anything to counter the almost hypnotic affect that breasts exerted over me. It seemed unfair that I should even have to deal with it–that it should be a problem in the first place.

Why should I be so disadvantaged due to their allure? I resented the fact that women had these "things" that had so much power over me.

Where was nature's balance? What did we have? What could I do?

I had to stop being taken over by women in general, and breasts in particular. That much was clear. I vowed to reverse the situation. I'd render them powerless. Simply change the equation: I will be in charge of myself, not them.

I drew up a plan of action in the "war room." This was serious stuff.

The battle plan: Decommission Their Armaments/Big Guns

The initial campaign (since this turned out to not be the end of it) consisted in my "not noticing them."

When I chanced upon a nice set of 'boobs' (please excuse my slang) in my range of vision, the instructions to myself were: Don't see them. Don't notice them. Filter them out.

It was OK to see them peripherally, (I instructed myself), to sort of glaze over them, not fully take them in. Concentrate more on the polyester or cotton fabric covering them. That was the idea. I simply would not let them enter the zoom room of my mind.

What I could see, what I would report to my mind was: "protruding mounds of flesh seen on person sitting at a desk." Or, "material blips appear on person walking by."

My mind didn't have a full deck to work with. There wasn't enough to get excited about or to desire a second look, as had always been the case previously.

I repeated this behavior for a few weeks, or maybe for a few months. It was a short campaign.

Part of me knew I was short-changing myself, if not outright lying to myself! It was as if I was doing a sleight of hand to myself.

A new strategy was hatched in the war room. Bombs away!

Second campaign: Rocket Propelled Launchers–Bomb the Boobs

I hesitate to mention this short-lived (thankfully) campaign. It entailed virtual violence and destruction. It brought up some lurking anger and resentment.

Let's be honest. I already mentioned that it seemed unfair that women should be able to "mess with my life," or meddle in my daily affairs, just by virtue of being female. By being a woman of the opposite sex. How unfair is that? Should they be able to render me helpless just because I looked at them? And I simply couldn't not look. My eyes gave me no choice in the matter.

I resented not being able to control myself simply because of some miss-placed torpedoes. My strategy: take them out! My guided missiles would simply seek the intended targets and eliminate them.

Now, instead of "not noticing them," I'd fix them with a laser focus and Bam! They were gone! Erased. The woman was still standing there, but breast-less. These were delicate rocket-propelled launchers. The later versions didn't even tear the blouse.

They were simply erased, no blood involved.

This macho, war-like strategy appealed to my base, revengeful side, but it was simply too gruesome and destructive to last beyond a few days or weeks (I hope it wasn't longer).

Third attempt: the One-Second Rule

This was a slight variation on the "don't notice" initial approach. And a welcome relief from the destructive previous campaign.

I had permission to look, not loiter. More of a fleeting glance than an actual hard look.

In practice, I'd notice her bust, then the eyes would snap back into straight ahead formation, off the boobs. Again, the eyes didn't have enough time to register the curvaceous waves of her blouse or sweater, nor savor the lovely skin exhibited in a low-cut top.

So difficult. Women have no idea what they put us through!

I couldn't do it at first. The temptation was too severe. I'd either find myself fastened to her spectacular orbs too long, or I'd look away fast enough, only to find my eyes jerked back to the target.

After a few weeks I achieved some success, and it became a habit in a matter of months, with an occasional backslide.

This campaign lasted five months. Then the time keeper got sloppy, let a few seconds slide here and there, and then the eyes lobbied for a permanent extension. The powerful imagination lobby backed up the eyes faction, and the one-second campaign whimpered to the finish line, defeated.

From the Neck Up

The previous campaigns were doomed to fail, given women's deep reserves, her vast arsenal. Again, how fair is that? What do we have? Diddley squat.

The guidelines were clear. Henceforth, my eyes would be permitted to only look at a woman from the neck up. Not the lower neck that starts to take in the shoulders. That was the first test case where the eyes lost decisively.

The plan was ingenious. And the challenge daunting.

Once I came up with this strategy, I sensed a winner. This could work. It was simple, elegant, had clean lines, and there wasn't wiggle room.

I could publicize it. I told my male friends about it, even my wife. She approved, though I sensed some doubt from her. My male friends understood the situation but seemed perplexed.

This new policy filled some loopholes from the previous campaigns. Since women have other, equally attractive parts: butt, hips, midriff, pelvis, legs—just to name a few, it's necessary to include these parts that can also cause collateral damage to the delicate male sensibility via their eyes.

I started slowly, taking on this momentous undertaking. It marked the beginning of a journey that would completely flip my "accepted" (at least what I was expected to accept) view of women. I couldn't have imagined the outcome, the new vistas that would open for me.

What a concept! From the neck up: My friends laughed at me. I laughed too. It was a funny idea, no doubt about it.

The first thing I noticed (to my relief) was, I was not pressured to do something *to her*. And instead of restricting myself, I allowed. I had permission to take in, to savor, to linger over a portion of a woman's anatomy that I had previously paid scant attention to.

The deprivation of not being allowed to see 75 to 85% of a woman's body was offset by being allowed to bask in her overlooked treasures, some "seen" for the first time.

It seemed unlikely at first, but gradually a woman's facial features became the main event, the star attraction. They suggested sexuality rather than broadcasting it. Her taken-for-granted sexual parts were ever so slowly receding into the background, almost unnoticed.

Her neck, chin and lips. So much expression in her lips. Then her chiseled cheeks and delicate nose, and ears set off by a simple, tiny pearl or a gigantic cowbell (well not quite! But some are extremely noticeable!). And the creme de la creme, her eyebrows, eyelashes and eyes. It's her eyes that can be scary, inviting, and foreboding all at the same time. Challenging.

This new world of women gradually opened to me in the following years.

At first, I missed the simple pleasure of watching a woman walking. Her gait, the natural sway of her hips, her posture that showcased her attire–all of it a parade of beauty in motion. But it was a relief to "not have to deal with it." In other words, absent was a need or desire to look again, to turn around, to get another gander at her derrière after she passed by.

The lopsided strategy of seeing a woman "from the neck up," initially necessary, gradually allowed a more balanced view. She could become a "new version" of herself, previously unseen.

Seeing a woman in her totality, as an actual person, diminishes and eventually can erase the compulsion of seeing a women's sexuality first.

Sometimes, sitting down with a few male acquaintances, having a cup of coffee, I would ask: "What's the first thing you think of when you see a pretty woman walk by?" After a few seconds of silence, a smile or smirk would spread over their face and the answer didn't need to be voiced.

After a few months, habit kicked in and I automatically begin to zero out the tendency to seek out the curves and contours of a woman's flesh, replace it with the ongoing new discovery of other, unnoticed charms.

Everything about a woman is charming. Every last detail from the nail on her little toe to the tint of her hair color and everything in between. Including her gestures, movements, her voice. The way she moves her body, dances, sings, laughs—all of it. All of her.

What I learned over a period of 25 years was a re-programming of my brain. My perceptions, the data or information I was forwarding to the brain, was at cross purposes with the old, automatic programming about how sexy she looked and wouldn't I like to bed her! But now, the linkage was different. My instincts were still intact, but they were being rerouted. Thankfully.

My neurons now had to find new pathways. Finally, I was taking tiny, baby steps toward recognizing the female sex as fully human beings.

I could now look at a woman walking by and not feel guilty. I was not using or abusing her in my mind sexually as before. I didn't burden my mind with sexual fantasies about her. Formerly I had thought that **I had to think about them that way.**

Miracles happened frequently. I'd catch the eye of a woman walking by, we'd engage for a second, exchange a look of recognition, maybe a smile, sometimes a greeting. She seemed to know that I was not judging her sexually, that sex was not on my mind. She sensed being seen as a person. No words were necessary to communicate this.

What joy to be able to connect with half of humanity that had been closed off for me! What riches! What incredible beauty they have. And that's just on the surface. Within each female lies untold riches, veins of gold.

Despite the progress I had made, I still surprised myself at times by being "taken in" once again, or should I say, "taken over," by a woman flaunting her sexuality. I was about 45 when I began this quest. About 20 years later, I came upon Eckhart Tolle's, *The Power of Now*. Reading it, I could see why I was still backsliding. Even though my view of women had been transformed, I would still find myself getting lost in sexualized thought-streams at times.

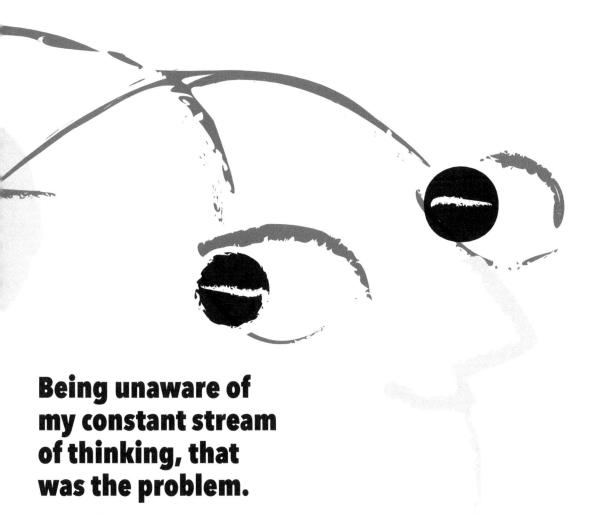

Being unaware of my constant stream of thinking, that was the problem.

This was the final piece: by paying attention to the times when I engaged in those thought streams, simply by becoming aware, I could stop the stream of thought for a moment and find peace.

Now

Women no longer scare me. They are first and foremost human beings, not sexual beings, certainly not sexual objects. A woman and I can be dancing, looking into each other's eyes and smiling, and sex is neither in the foreground or the background. That's incredible!

On the other hand, I am still a male sexual being. No less interested than before, and maybe even more so. But more tuned-in to their overall beauty,

as well as their curvaceous bodies. They're still attractive and alluring.

I'm still looking, but it's looking with appreciation and admiration, more than desire. I am observing nature's own living artworks. Looking while tempered in joy can be an end in itself.

The patriarchal, sexualized construct of the world has "enjoyed" a 10,000 year run. It's time to take it apart, and rebuild a New World together. The result cannot be but magical.

Attention

Intro

You already have a story. You are a story, assembled since birth with input you inherited and input from the culture that surrounded you, that cultured you.

That culture is patriarchal in nature. Women understand they have to "buck" the patriarchal system to "get anywhere." Women have been clawing their way forward for thousands of years, attempting to break through men's barricaded citadel on-a-hill. It's now men's turn—to upend the patriarchal tables, to free ourselves, and to welcome women to the "Club."

Competing with that story is the underlying story: **consciousness**.

Our true nature is consciousness, the awareness that this body that we walk around in disguises our true Self. No matter how lost/ lonely/hopeless or hapless we feel, we can always come back to the *present moment* and be aware that, "Yes, I am conscious. That other story is not who I am."

The challenge is overcoming inertia, the result of our programming. We get used to believing and behaving certain ways, and we're convinced that that's the right way. Our neural pathways have been wired to accept or reject information depending on whether it meets our stories' criteria. It's scary to question those assumptions. It's not called "comfort" zone for nothing.

But once you dip your toes into even the shallow tide pools of consciousness/ awareness, you will see you won't sink, and you will soon take the plunge.

THE ROLE OF

Inertia

Chapter 22

The mind, conditioned by the past, always seeks to re-create what it knows and what it is familiar with. Even if it's painful, it's "like family." As Eckhart Tolle says, "The mind always adheres to the known." (*The Power of Now***)**

That explains why we continue to make the same mistakes—even to the point of watching ourselves doing it, knowing the outcome won't be good: walking into a pole/pit/post/person, or a car!

We even find it difficult to choose a healthy body over one prone to disease. "I deserve that bag of Snickers and stop snickering or I'll dump this bowl of sugar on your head!" We get used to having headaches, colds, indigestion, insomnia, bypasses and overpasses, and our minds say, "It's normal; misery is normal." Let's stick with that.

As we've seen before, the daily news is, "All the news that fits your fears." It's news of the world, filled with fear-driven anecdotes, stories, half-truths, and non-truths. The news that we see and hear functions as a baby blanket to keep us swaddled in the information that we need to believe, if we are to keep being swindled. In other words, to keep the patriarchal corporate machine rolling.

If our story doesn't include finding out what we are doing here, we're living a half-life.

If we don't realize our identity, we are adrift in a sea of plastic flotsam, those vast pools of debris in dead ocean waters.

But if we can get past the inertia blocks and the story we've inherited, we can sense what consciousness feels like, experience the joy of a morning walk while noticing plants and stones for the first time. We can learn to relish ourselves as waves, as ripples on the surface of the ocean, knowing that our role as ripples *entails being part of the very ocean that forms the ripples.*

Chapter 23

It often happens that someone receives a book from a friend who hopes the book will help them to "see the light."

The person reads a few sentences – it could've been *A Road Less Traveled, The Power of Now,* or *The Untethered Soul* – and wonders about the psychic make-up of their friend, after they toss the book aside. Five or ten years later, they pick up the same book and wonder about the psyche of the person who tossed it earlier. **Now** it makes sense.

My experience was different.

I'd been married about 25 years when I attended a high school class reunion in 2008. I mentioned to a classmate that our marriage had gone a "little stale." He asked if I had read *The Power of Now.* Back in Long Beach, I checked it out of the library, opened it, read a few sentences, and felt like I'd been clobbered by a 2 x 4 across my forehead.

"Your thoughts are not real."

The whole foundation of the edifice/story that I'd constructed for years – the case against my wife – suddenly crumbled in about five sentences.

All the mantras I had repeated over and over in my mind – you can do better/be better/have more/deserve more/better sex – all of it suddenly went up in flames. My mind, my own thinking mind that I believed in, trusted in – had been serving up an enticing platter of thoughts, embellished by false tidbits from the Hollywood world of fantasy and media myths from the daily news. It had become *My Story,* a story shot through with patriarchal messaging.

My wife was not the problem. I had given license to my mind to come up with a narrative to explain, "Why am I not happy with her?" My mind ran with it! I could've written a book with all the material my silly, out of control mind was digging up. It all seemed to make sense. And it looked like my only option was to leave. That's how crazy it/I was getting.

I believed my thoughts were **real**.

New Story

Chapter 24

You now have an idea of how your story fits into the grand scheme of things. You see the play of forces throughout history and the role that your gender–whether male or female–played in your story. Life is the dancer; you are the dance.

Your new story begins when you sense something is different. It can be an "aha" moment, or perhaps you read something that jars your sensibility, makes you aware of something new, something you hadn't thought of before.

You might read: "Stillness allows an inner space to open up within you," and that stops your thinking mind for a moment. In that gap of a few seconds, you sense **presence**. That could display itself in your mind as the opposite, as **absence**–because for a few seconds your mind is empty, drained of thoughts. That could be terrifying! For a couple of seconds your story/identity is annihilated. Or you might be looking up at the night sky, and for a second your mind stops thinking. Again, scary, but also invigorating, opening a new canvas/page to explore.

In both those instances you touch a vein of knowing within yourself. You have an untapped reservoir of *deep knowledge*. You don't need a guru. It's all within you, waiting to be tapped at the right moment.

Up until that moment everything continues as it always has. And, we do not have a choice in that state. When we're in the grip of thinking, which is the norm for most of humanity, we're not free to choose. Choices are being made for us–by our conditioned minds–and our minds are conditioned by patriarchy.

We may think we're choosing because that's what we've been told. But we have been programming those choices by previous choices, previous programming and conditioning. We are on a hamster wheel, looking as though we are making progress, but really running in circles with the same programming running through our heads…

We're not thinking our thoughts. They're thinking us.

When I chose to walk out on my wife one day, I was not in charge of that decision. My mind had been programming me for that decision for a long time. It wasn't what "I" really wanted to do. I changed my mind by late afternoon.

If you're comfortable in your life and feel no need to change, that's fine. If you're ready to make a change it will find you, if you're alert. That's how the universe works. Sometimes we must re-enroll in the course called "suffering" before we're ready. It could be a "crash course."

NOW IS THE

Right Time

Chapter 25

If you're having any doubts about whether this is the right time for you to embark on a new journey/story, welcome aboard. You might as well jump in. If you're reading this, you're probably ready. Unplug your TV. Plug into your inner, knowing *Self*.

We are at a particular juncture in the evolution of our species that is critical to the survival of our species. By joining in, you are becoming an important part of that.

Everyone has a part to play in the unfolding drama. Consciousness is increasing on a personal and on a collective level. It is deepening, getting stronger, to meet an also-evolving new force which threatens to take control of mankind or possibly destroy it.

The male principle–the horizontal, the Yang–has gone wild in a small, well positioned, wealthy group of human beings, predominantly male. It's a perfect example of how seemingly rational, well-intentioned (in their minds) humans can simply go off their rational rails. Innocent of wisdom, they succumb to thought-controlled, ego-distorted "reality."

This is truly the "rotten fruit" that the patriarchal tree is now offering.

Each of us is capable of that "mad scientist" thinking. They are not an evil, separate species, even though they are perpetrating evil deeds galore. They are also attempting to re-create our species into a new one, created in the image of AI, artificial intelligence.

The exciting (and good) news is that we're gaining momentum to transform the human species–from one that has been controlled by our thinking minds, to one that is able to *use our minds to think* and not be used (and abused) by thinking.

This is an incredible time to be alive. A transitional time to the New Earth.

The even better news is we don't have to wait for the transformation to take place. Once we've begun our journey, in a sense we're there! It's taken hold within us and we're already reflecting it back in/on our new world. We are emanating vibrations that resonate with the power of the Universe to create the New Earth. Join in!

You are not

YOUR STORY

—

Chapter 26

When we are born to our parents, we inherit their story. This includes their genetic schemes and the cultural influences that they inherited. This means we acquire their beliefs, customs, superstitions, food tastes and even everyday living habits.

If we are attached to those beliefs, then we are identified with our story. We think it is who we are and we think it defines us. We know we are identified with our story when someone questions our beliefs, and we feel attacked. It's hard to change our story when *we've established it as our identity*.

Our beliefs, whatever they happen to be, are considered "sacred" and some people are willing to die to uphold them, no matter how crazy they might be—there is or isn't a Devil, killing ants is the same as homicide, male sperm is a potential baby so masturbation should be outlawed, breast milk should be processed like regular milk to make sure it's safe—as preposterous as they might be.

I recall a time (probably in my 30's) when I had some beliefs about the world and reality.

I distinctly remember feeling so strongly about them I was willing to die for them (and now I don't even remember what they were).

But beliefs are just thoughts. They have no reality.

Our identity—our story—is not who we are. The story we keep alive by our thoughts is just a set of beliefs that trigger emotions, and our life is subsequently circumscribed within that construct. It's not a wrong way to live and many live their entire lives that way. We may die upholding our story, but it's not who or what we are. If we are not our beliefs and our story, what are we?

A shining, brilliant star in the cosmos, our potential unlimited by space or time, our being is a part of Being itself, our consciousness is a part of the consciousness of every person we know, alive or dead, as well as plants and animals. We're not the sun but a ray of the sun.

As close to being
God as we can get
without actually
being God!

Afterword

**We're on a breathtaking journey.
On a breath-giving one as well.**

There is neither a beginning nor an end to it.

We could say it begins at birth and every day is a new birth, a rebirth.

We travel along the horizontal path of our everyday life, following our prescribed script, until we get to the vertical dimension. There time stops.

Our human story that has made up our life simply melts into the *be* of Being.

In that realm we are beyond story, beyond reality. We no longer have *a* life, we *are* life.

When we realize that we are life, all the boundaries and walls that separated us from each other and from nature, simply dissolve.

We look to the sun. It ignites the joy in our bodies as surely as do the eyes of a baby.

We dance, our bodies transformed and enveloped in love.

~~~

The Author

Then I stumbled onto *The Power Of Now* in 2008, at a critical juncture of my life. Suddenly it all became clear–my lifetime quest for the answer. *Thinking,* that's the problem. Not sex, not patriarchy–but thinking that engendered them and partnered to twist them. The thinking that keeps us from finding the "stillness within" which yields the answers to our questions.

From Patriarchy to Paradise offers further reflections on our sexual nature as males and females. I offer a personal journey of exploring the sexual intersection of patriarchy and masculinity: women's breasts.

Life continues to be a bold, adventure-filled journey, the thrill of not knowing what's around the corner–is there even a corner? And the joy of human beings. We are witnessing the re-birth of ourselves and the Earth.

It was after my second wife died from Alzheimer's in 2018 that I began writing again.

I have two adult children and four grandkids from my first wife, two stepchildren and four grandkids from my second wife. I now make my home in Long Beach, CA.

I was born in Cut Bank, Montana in 1940. The Blackfoot Indian Reservation begins at the western edge of town and extends into Glacier National Park. It offers some mountainous vistas. The Blackfeet showed me interior ones.

My best friend at Saint Margaret Grade School was "Beaver" Bird. Looking back, there was a stillness or presence about him that made it easy to be around him. He had an easy smile, like his mother "Winnie," who often erupted into laughter.

It's possible that he awoke some dormant feeling in me, some sense of the possibilities that life has to offer.

Throughout my life, I've tried to make sense of it, given the data at hand. In high school, I concluded that sex turned the wheels of Cut Bank.

By the time I retired from teaching in 2000, I had concluded that Patriarchy was the main problem of sex, for both men and women. I wrote a book about how women have been treated throughout history.

This book is a collaborative effort between me, the illustrator, Gabriel Berron, the designer, Anne Pace, and the editor, Melinda Tourangeau. She entered the project, almost as an afterthought, but helped to redirect and transform the book into a coherent whole. They deserve equal credit for the final product. As well as fitting together Gabriel Berron's illustrations with the text, Anne often comes up with a different word or phrase that invariably improves the meaning of what I am trying to convey. Gabriel's illustrations have improved with each book (his third, Anne's fourth).

We meet on zoom, almost on a weekly basis, when we are "in production." Gabriel is in Mexico City, Anne is in Vermont, Melinda's in New Hampshire, and I am in Southern California.

I hope you enjoy this book as much as we have enjoyed working on it.

Jerry Schaefer

Learn more and see Jerry's previous books at:
www.expandjoy.com

LOOK INSIDE